CARS
T-BIRD

Michael Bradley

mc **Marshall Cavendish**
Benchmark
New York

Marshall Cavendish Benchmark
99 White Plains Road
Tarrytown, NY 10591
www.marshallcavendish.us

Library of Congress Cataloging-in-Publication Data

Bradley, Michael, 1962—
T-bird / by Michael Bradley.
p. cm. — (Cars)
Includes bibliographical references and index.
ISBN 978-0-7614-2983-8
1. Thunderbird automobile—History—Juvenile literature. I. Title.
TL215.T46B73 2009
629.222'2—dc22
2007041249

Photo research by Connie Gardner

Cover photo by © Ron Kimball Stock Photography/Ron Kimball

The photographs in this book are used by permission and through the courtesy of: *Ron Kimball/www.kimballstock.
com*: back cover, 1, 20, 28, 29; *From the Collection of the Henry Ford Museum*: 3, 14, 16, 18 (T and B), 21; *The Everett
Collection*: 4; *Corbis*: Car Culture, 7; Bruce Benedict/Transtock, 8; Bettmann, 10, 11, 19; Tom Brakefield, 12; *Getty
Images*: Car Culture, 13; *AP Photo*: 15, 23, 25, 26 (T and B), *The Image Works*: Topham, 17.

Publisher: Michelle Bisson
Art Director: Anahid Hamparian
Series Designer: Daniel Roode

Printed in Malaysia
1 3 5 6 4 2

CONTENTS

The 1955 Thunderbird was the ultimate muscle car. From its hooded headlights to its tailfins, the T-Bird looked cool and moved fast.

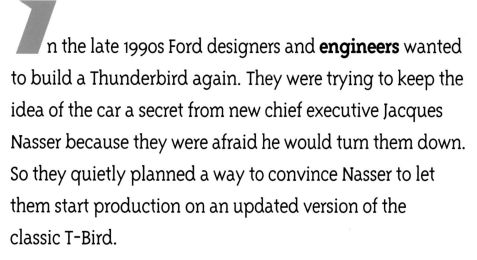

CHAPTER ONE
A CLASSIC AT ANY TIME

In the late 1990s Ford designers and **engineers** wanted to build a Thunderbird again. They were trying to keep the idea of the car a secret from new chief executive Jacques Nasser because they were afraid he would turn them down. So they quietly planned a way to convince Nasser to let them start production on an updated version of the classic T-Bird.

Ford had stopped producing the T-Bird in 1997 because of poor sales. The vehicle that had **debuted** in 1955 as a "personal luxury car" was **eclipsed** by other models that were more current. But they were never the cultural **icon** the T-Bird had been.

Anybody who saw the 1973 movie *American Graffiti* knew how much magic the Thunderbird brought. One of the main characters, Curt, spends much of the film trying to find a girl who is cruising the streets of his town in a white T-Bird. She and the car were symbols of what was cool and beautiful. That was the Thunderbird.

In the 1997 movie *Flubber*, special effects artists were able to make it look as if Robin Williams was behind the wheel of a flying T-Bird. Getting a classic T-Bird off the ground in real life is tough—the car weighs more than three tons!

And now, in quiet meeting rooms and lonely offices, some people at Ford wanted it back. And, you know what? Nasser said yes. In fact, he was an **enthusiastic** backer of the project. Imagine that. There would have to be some changes made and some **accommodations** to keep costs down. But Thunderbird, Take Two, was a go.

It was an exciting time, but most of Thunderbird's life had been exciting. From the first concepts in the early 1950s through its reintroduction in 2001, the car was a symbol of Ford's power and style.

Originally conceived to rival Chevrolet's Corvette, the Thunderbird was a combination of cool and speed, thanks to its distinctive design and its strong power source that was made to give drivers speed and great handling.

The 1956 T-Bird convertible featured rear porthole windows in its removable hardtop.

Throughout its first life the Thunderbird grew from a cool two-seater into a super-sized four-passenger model. As the decades moved on, the Thunderbird changed and adapted. Ford made adjustments to increase fuel economy and to reduce the size when smaller cars became popular. Despite the various **phases** it went through, Thunderbird stayed true to its initial goal of bringing luxury to customers while still providing an exciting ride.

The 2002 Thunderbird was a modern-looking car with some classic design elements, including a wide front grill, porthole windows, and round headlights.

When that 2002 version of Thunderbird debuted, it featured design elements of the classic T-Birds, while still giving its drivers the most modern comforts. Some thought it was an odd combination, but Thunderbird had always been about that. The Ford advertising team focused on the personal luxury in that first car because it set the T-Bird apart from its competition. The Thunderbird always tried to be more than just a good-looking ride. It was comfortable. For a while there, it was big. Really big. And when it entered the twenty-first century, it did so as the perfect combination of old-school style and new-world ease. Those secret meetings could have been held in the middle of the Ford lunchroom, with **megaphones** announcing every idea, because the Thunderbird was always a winner.

Henry Ford II, whose grandfather started the Ford Motor Company, was responsible for hiring the designer of the Thunderbird and led the company for thirty-five years.

The **pioneer** was gone. Henry Ford, the man who had introduced the automobile to the American public, died in 1947, and his grandson, Henry Ford II, had taken over. It was a time of great **creativity**, since the younger Ford was not as **conservative** as his grandfather had been. He wanted sharper looks for his vehicles. He wanted a new style.

So, he hired Franklin Q. Hershey, who had worked under legendary designer Harley Earl. Hershey's mission was simple: to update the Ford line. One of his first challenges was to come up with a response to Chevrolet's popular new Corvette, which debuted in 1953. That answer was the Thunderbird convertible, which Ford introduced to the world in February 1954 at the Detroit Auto Show.

People flocked to dealerships in 1955 to check out the Thunderbird, which was available with a ragtop or a removable hardtop.

The 1957 T-Bird was the last two-seater model until the 2002 Retrobird.

There are three stories about how the car got its name. The first is that it was the brainstorm of a contest winner, who won a new pair of pants and $95 for his idea. The second is that it came from the name of an **exclusive** Palm Springs, California, housing development called Thunderbird Heights. The final tale is that it was named for the **mythic** American Indian creature, which caused thunder by beating its wings and lightning when it blinked its eyes.

Whatever the case, the two-seater Thunderbird was an instant success. In fact, the first day the car arrived in showrooms, four thousand people left deposits for the T-Bird. Talk about your big first impressions.

And why wouldn't people want a piece of it? The T-Bird had a powerful **V-8 engine** with standard power brakes, steering, and windows. There was wall-to-wall carpeting inside, a shiny chrome bumper, and a choice of two roofs—a convertible **ragtop** or a hardtop that could be removed. It had a wraparound windshield, hooded headlights, and tailfins, all of which were common for the time. But this was no tiny sports car. It was a hulking roadster that weighed nearly 3,400 pounds (1,542 kilograms). It was also a sales Goliath, logging 16,155 purchases during its first year, compared with just 700 for the Corvette. Ford had faced a big test and had aced it.

Ford Motor Company wanted the T-Bird to be a fast car, so every car came equipped with a powerful V-8 engine.

The next couple of years allowed Ford to refine the classic Thunderbird look by adding porthole windows in the back and by expanding the trunk, giving the car a longer, more impressive body. It continued to outsell the Corvette, but it wasn't selling well enough.

The 1958 T-Bird was even bigger than the first models—it had a back seat and could fit four people. Even more impressive was the retractable ragtop, which disappeared into the trunk.

New Ford executive Robert McNamara wasn't happy. Even though the T-Bird had done well, those in charge before him had not expected it to be a big moneymaker. In fact, Ford called it a Halo Car. That meant it was something of an angel, a car that helped other models sell by drawing customers into showrooms. McNamara wanted more than just a car that did good deeds. He wanted it to make money, so the two-seater model was replaced by a four-seater, which would appeal to families. It was longer and wider than the previous model, and it debuted in February 1958. Was it a success? Well, *Motor Trend* named it "Car of the Year." Not bad. And it would get better.

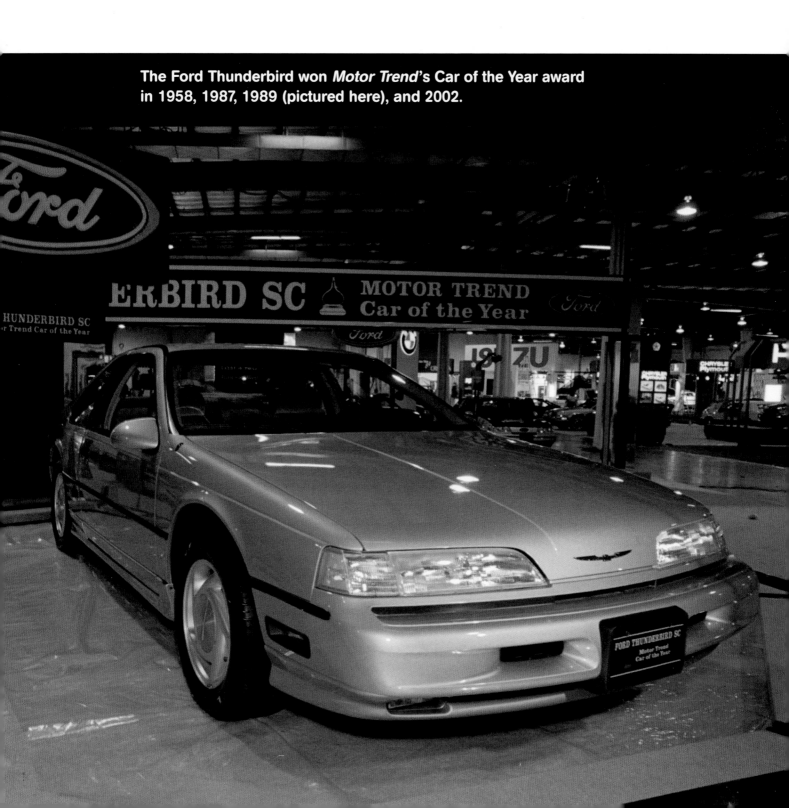

The Ford Thunderbird won *Motor Trend*'s Car of the Year award in 1958, 1987, 1989 (pictured here), and 2002.

In 1961 the Thunderbird was selected as the official pace car of the Indianapolis 500's Golden Anniversary run. All thirty-four cars provided by Ford to the Indy 500 were painted a special shade of gold.

next generations

It was the fiftieth year of the Indianapolis Motor Speedway, the Golden **Anniversary**, and the folks there needed a special way to celebrate. They wanted that year's **pace car** for the Indy 500 to be the perfect partner for the grand race track.

Of course, they chose the Thunderbird. The 1961 model was outfitted with **decals** and special paint, and it drove—top down, of course—out in front of the drivers as they prepared for America's famous race. It was the perfect way to introduce the newest generation of T-Bird to America.

GOLDEN ANNIVERSARY

INDIANAPOLIS MOTOR SPEEDWAY
MAY 30, 1961

Thunderbird convertibles cruise around Washington, D.C., during the Inauguration Day parade for President John F. Kennedy.

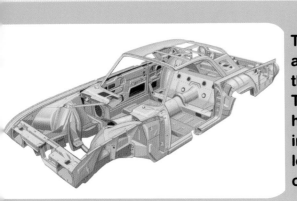

Though only a two-seater, the 1961 Thunderbird had an impressively long chassis, or frame.

It was certainly a sharp-looking car, especially in convertible form. It still had the long, flat back deck. Up front, the V-8 power remained. People who wondered if it provided enough personal luxury only needed to check out the **Inauguration Day** parade in Washington, D.C. When Robert McNamara stepped down as Ford chief to become the secretary of defense under newly elected president John F. Kennedy, the company sent twenty-five Thunderbird convertibles for VIPs to use at the celebration. If that didn't give the car an **image** of class and style, nothing could.

The 1962 T-Bird had a more rounded body than earlier models and was nicknamed "Rocket Bird."

The 1960s were good for the T-Bird, which continued to stake out its claim as the country's top choice for comfort and power. In 1963 Ford adopted the advertising **slogan** "Unique in all the World" about the T-Bird. Its distinctive look grew when Princess Grace of Monaco gave her ideas for a special Princess Grace model that year. In 1965, for its tenth anniversary, Ford created a special edition Ford T-Bird with a one-of-a-kind **landau** roof. In 1967 the convertible was discontinued, but sales increased as the car's rich personality attracted a wider audience.

During the 1960s auto manufacturers produced "fake convertible" models, which had vinyl roofs and no rear windows. Though this 1966 Thunderbird Town Landau looks like a convertible, the roof cannot be removed.

As the 1970s dawned, the Thunderbird had established itself as a popular choice for middle-age drivers. But these drivers wanted even more comfort, so the car was made bigger and bigger in the first few years of the decade. Ford told people it was "More Thunderbird Than Ever," and it sure was. The car had a larger body and more room inside. It also had a problem **looming** on the horizon: the gas crunch. As prices rose, and fuel economy became important, Thunderbird faced declining sales. So, it became smaller again.

The 1983 Thunderbird offered buyers power, style, and modern technology. Among the custom features were keyless entry and voice-alert systems.

But not less stylish. The 1977 T-Bird lacked the length and weight of its older brothers, but it still came in sixteen different exterior colors and had twelve types of roof to choose from. It was popular and sold well, in part because it was less expensive than other Thunderbird models.

Since 1913, the Ford Motor Company has been using an assembly line to produce cars and trucks. Here, in 1960, grills wait to be installed on T-Birds.

The Thunderbird's twenty-fifth anniversary came in 1980, but some of the car's appeal seemed to have been lost. The press wasn't too happy with the latest version, and sales sagged. The car that had defined the top end of Ford's line was struggling, and it needed a little help. So, Ford engineers went back to the old days. The 1983 T-Bird Turbo **Coupe** had two seats and a more powerful engine. America noticed. Three times as many Thunderbirds were sold in 1983 as in the year before. It would be the start of a strong run for T-Bird but also the beginning of the end.

For a while.

CHAPTER FOUR
BACK FOR MORE

The decision was made. Thunderbird was ending its run as Ford's longest-lasting model. Sales had dropped on the T-Bird, which could no longer deliver the same top-shelf luxury it once had.

The last car would roll off the line in 1997, and the company had a big decision to make. Who would get the final T-Bird? It couldn't go to just anyone, because it needed to be preserved and cherished. So, Ford had a contest to see who deserved to own the car. The winner, Classic Thunderbird Club International in Signal Hill, California, was chosen to receive it and preserve it.

There was a quiet ceremony at the Lorain, Ohio, assembly plant, as the laser red T-Bird rolled off the line. It had a rear **spoiler** and

Talk about brand new! These 1997 T-Birds roll off the assembly line at an Ohio Ford plant.

15-inch (38 cm) chrome wheels. As executives and factory workers looked on, they couldn't help but wonder how it had come to this. How had a forty-two-year-old symbol of Ford design ended up in the history books but not the showroom?

The answer was sagging sales. Even though the Turbo Coupe had been popular in the 1980s, and the Super Coupe had taken Ford into the 1990s with good **horsepower** and styling, American drivers weren't enthusiastic. There were more luxury choices available to them, so they looked elsewhere. As the late 1990s dawned, the longest-running Ford product of all time was finished.

Or so we thought.

That's when the whispering started. And the secret meetings. Before long, Ford had made a **commitment** to the Thunderbird again. The new model would be a complete step back to the T-Bird's high-flying roots. In fact, it borrowed from many different models. It would have a totally hidden convertible roof or a removable **fiberglass** top with a porthole, just like the late 1950s cars did. In 1999 Ford displayed a **prototype** at the Detroit Auto Show, and people flipped. They couldn't wait to get their hands on this new/old T-Bird.

How crazy was it? Deliveries were scheduled for the summer of 2001, but dealers were taking deposits on the new T-Bird eighteen months ahead of schedule. Some people paid extra for the cars.

In 1999 designers for Ford based the new Thunderbird on the original models from the 1950s. The concept car (shown here) generated excitement and people were ordering the T-Birds even before they appeared in dealers' showrooms in 2001.

The black 2002 Neiman-Marcus Limited Edition T-Bird featured a removable silver roof. It took only two hours to sell all two hundred cars, which cost more than $40,000 each.

Ford celebrated the T-Bird's fiftieth anniversary by creating a 2005 Thunderbird convertible in a limited edition cashmere color. This anniversary model sits next to a light blue 1957 T-Bird.

They did so to make sure they would get one of the first cars. The car looked like a 1955 Thunderbird shot into the future, with a rounded front and circular headlights and taillights. The car had a V-8 engine and leather interior. It was the perfect way for the Thunderbird to come back. The upscale retail store Neiman-Marcus put a special edition in its 2000 Christmas catalog, and all two hundred models were sold in one day. Clearly, America was ready for the new T-Bird.

The first year of sales proved that. Ford had hoped to sell 25,000, but it moved more than 31,000—a great start. After that, though, enthusiasm for the "Retrobird" slowed. Only 14,506 moved out of showrooms in 2003, and by 2005 only 9,220 T-Birds were sold. What began as an exciting new idea had fizzled.

But that couldn't change Thunderbird's exciting fifty-year history. It had gone from a personal luxury car to a hot symbol of twenty-first-century cool, with plenty of stops along the way. Thunderbird was an American classic, and even though it ended its run in 2005, those who owned one will never forget it.

Vital Statistics

1955 Ford Thunderbird

Power: 198 hp
Engine Size: 292 ci/4.8L
Engine Type: Mercury V-8
Weight: 2,833 lbs (1,285 kg)
Top Speed: 112 mph (180 km/h)
0–60 mph (0–96.5 km/h): 11.5 sec

2002 Ford Thunderbird

Power: 252 hp
Engine Size: 241 ci/3.9L
Engine Type: V-8
Weight: 3,746 lbs (1,699 kg)
Top Speed: 138 mph (222 km/h)
0–60 mph (0–96.5 km/h): 7 sec

GLOSSARY

accommodation	A change or adaptation to suit someone or something else's needs.
anniversary	The annual celebration of a special event.
commitment	A pledge or promise.
conservative	Following traditional methods and views; unlikely to take risks.
coupe	A smaller, enclosed car that usually seats two people.
creativity	The ability to imagine things and then produce them.
decal	A picture or design that can be stuck onto various things, including a car or truck.
debut	The first appearance of something in public.
eclipse	To overtake in importance or popularity.
engineer	A person who develops plans and designs for roads, bridges, automotive products, etc.
enthusiastic	Having or showing intense interest or desire.
exclusive	Limited to one person or small group of people.
fiberglass	A product that is made from extremely thin fibers of glass to create a material that can be used many ways, including forming the body of an automobile.
horsepower	A measure of the power generated by a motor or engine. The greater the horsepower (hp), the higher the speed at which an automobile is able to travel.
icon	A symbol that is highly respected.
image	The public idea of a person, product, or company.
inauguration day	The day a new president is sworn into office.
landau	A vinyl roof on a car that gives it the look of a convertible.
looming	Threatening danger in the near future.
megaphone	A cone-shaped object use to make a person's voice louder.

mythic	Existing only in legend or fiction.
pace car	A car that leads the competing race cars through a warm-up lap, but does not take part in the race.
phases	The parts of a plan or project.
pioneer	One who goes somewhere or does something before others do.
prototype	The first model developed that is the pattern for all others.
ragtop	The cloth roof on a convertible that can be removed or retracted.
slogan	A catchy phrase used to generate interest in a product or political candidate.
spoiler	A device attached to the trunk of a car to give cars a steadier ride by lessening the air around the auto.
V-8 engine	A powerful engine that has eight cylinders to make a large vehicle move quickly.

FURTHER INFORMATION

BOOKS

Long, Brian. *The Book of the Ford Thunderbird From 1954*. Dorchester, England: Veloce Publishing, 2007.

Mueller, Mike. *Thunderbird Milestones*. St. Paul, MN: MBI Publishing Company, 2003.

Taft, Alan H. *Thunderbird Fifty Years*. St. Paul, MN: Motorbooks International, 2004.

WEB SITES

www.intl-tbirdclub.com

www.tbird.org

www.tbirdfans.com

Page numbers in **boldface** are photographs.

About the Author

MICHAEL BRADLEY is a writer and broadcaster who lives near Philadelphia. He has written for *Sports Illustrated for Kids, Hoop, Inside Stuff*, and *Slam* magazines and is a regular contributor to Comcast SportsNet in Philadelphia.